Vanity Fair

WILLIAM MAKEPEACE THACKERAY

Level 3

Retold by Pauline Francis
Series Editors: Andy Hopkins and Jocelyn Potter

Pearson Education Limited
Edinburgh Gate, Harlow,
Essex CM20 2JE, England
and Associated Companies throughout the world.

ISBN: 978-1-4058-6237-0

First published by Penguin Books 2000
This edition published 2008

3 5 7 9 10 8 6 4 2

Text copyright © Penguin Books Ltd 2000
This edition copyright © Pearson Education Ltd 2008

Typeset by Graphicraft Ltd, Hong Kong
Set in 11/14pt Bembo
Printed in China
SWTC/02

Published by Pearson Education Ltd in association with
Penguin Books Ltd, both companies being subsidiaries of Pearson Plc

Acknowledgement:
Photographs © BBC Worldwide 1998

Loughborough
COLLEGE est 1909

For a complete list of the titles available in the Penguin Readers series please write to your local
Pearson Longman office or to: Penguin Readers Marketing Department, Pearson Education,
Edinburgh Gate, Harlow, Essex CM20 2JE, England.

Contents

Introduction

She promised to love her friend for ever and ever and ever before she counted the money from kind Mr Sedley. Then, crying, she left. As the carriage turned the corner, Rebecca immediately dried her eyes. She began to think about Sir Pitt. 'Will he wear fine clothes?' she asked herself. 'Will he be very proud? I do not think that I have ever met a baronet!'

Rebecca (Becky) Sharp works at a school for young ladies until, at the age of seventeen, she is given the job of governess at the home of Sir Pitt Crawley. Before she goes to the Crawleys' house, she stays with her friend Amelia Sedley. Amelia comes from a good family and she is in love with an army officer. Becky does not have any money or a family to help her, but she is strong and intelligent. What kind of life will she and Amelia have after they leave Miss Pinkerton's school? Will they find problems and sadness, or love and happiness? Which of them is prepared for real life?

William Makepeace Thackeray, the writer of this book, was born in 1811 and became one of the most important names in English literature in the 1800s. He was born in India and lived there when he was a child. Like Joseph Sedley in *Vanity Fair*, his father was a 'collector' – he was the governor of a large area of the country, and he collected money for the British East India Company.

Thackeray was sent home to England in 1817 to go to school. Then he went to Cambridge University, but he did not complete his studies there. He became the friend of young writers like Edward Fitzgerald and Tennyson, and on his travels in Europe he met the writer Goethe at Weimar. Thackeray began to study law in 1831, but he was not interested in this field and never worked in it. He also studied art, and later he started to write for newspapers. Through this work, he met more of the important writers around London at that time. When he had no more money, he moved to Paris. He lived there from 1833–37. First, he tried to work as a painter and then he worked for a newspaper. He also travelled widely.

Thackeray returned to London with his first wife, Isabella Shawe, and wrote for a number of magazines. From 1842, he wrote for the magazine *Punch*. He became famous for making fun of the lives of rich people. He attacked people who wanted to seem important – people like George Osborne's father in *Vanity Fair*. These attacks were serious, but they were also amusing.

In the same way, in *Vanity Fair* (1848), Thackeray suggests, with a smile, what he does not like about people. He does not say that George Osborne, for example, is a bad man. We are told that, in Amelia's eyes, Osborne is 'the bravest and most beautiful man in the British army, in Europe, in the world.' The writer continues: 'And it is possible that Lieutenant Osborne thought so too.'

Thackeray never tells us that Becky Sharp is a bad woman. But we understand her from early in the book. Mr Sedley kindly gives her a present of some money, and she counts it. She cries when she leaves her friend's house. But then her carriage turns the corner and she stops crying immediately. When men enter her life, she has plans for them. And it seems that nothing can stop her plans.

The Snobs of England (1847) is a collection of Thackeray's work for *Punch* magazine. After *Vanity Fair*, he continued writing books and short stories like *Pendennis* (1850), *Henry Esmond* (1852), *The Newcomes* (1855) and *The Virginians* (1857–9). Thackeray died suddenly from heart trouble at Christmas in 1863 before he could finish his last book, *Denis Duval*. Today his work is studied because of his clear understanding of people and because of his amusing descriptions of their lives and their search for success.

Vanity Fair has always been Thackeray's most popular work of fiction. The title comes from John Bunyan's book *The Pilgrim's Progress* (1678). In Bunyan's book, Christian has to pass through a town, Vanity, where there is a market all year. The market is called 'Vanity Fair'. At Vanity Fair, people sell things that are not really important – fine houses, important positions, titles. It is interesting that the success of *Vanity Fair* earned a lot of money and a good position for Thackeray in the world of literature.

So the title of Thackeray's book is very important to the story. In the world of his book, everyone wants these amusing but unimportant things. They will do anything to get them.

The time of *Vanity Fair* was not long before Thackeray wrote the story. In 1812, Napoleon Bonaparte turned back from Moscow because of the terrible Russian winter. His armies then had to fight the armies of Prussia, Russia, Britain and Sweden. At the battle of Leipzig, in October 1813, the French lost to armies that were twice as big. When Napoleon's enemies arrived in Paris, he was sent to rule the island of Elba. Then, in March 1815, Napoleon returned to France. The first part of the story of *Vanity Fair* takes place at the time of the Battle of Waterloo in June, 1815. This was the battle that ended the war.

When *Vanity Fair* came out in 1847, in monthly parts, everyone was interested in Becky Sharp. She is the main reason for our enjoyment of the book now. Her plans for the future are clever. She is free from the fear of doing wrong. She always knows what she wants. And she works hard to get it.

It is also interesting that Thackeray, the writer of the book, seems to talk to the reader; the story is told to a listener. After Rebecca becomes a governess at the Crawleys' home, Queen's Crawley, the writer tells us, 'We have now met the more important persons in the family, so we must think about Rebecca.'

And later, when he introduces a new person into the story, 'It is time now to meet Miss Crawley.'

And now it is time for you to meet the people of *Vanity Fair*.

Chapter 1 Leaving School

There were two young ladies in the carriage that was leaving Miss Pinkerton's excellent school.

Amelia Sedley had a letter from Miss Pinkerton to Mr and Mrs Sedley, and a copy of Johnson's Dictionary with Miss Pinkerton's signature inside.

You must know immediately that Amelia was a dear little person. She is not a heroine, so I do not need to describe her. I can tell you that her nose was too short for a heroine. Her face was too round. But she had a very nice smile, and her eyes were bright and happy-looking. They were too often full of tears, it is true. She was the kindest young lady in the world.

The other young lady in the carriage, Miss Rebecca Sharp, had no letter from Miss Pinkerton. And no Johnson's Dictionary – but more of that very soon.

Miss Sharp's father taught drawing at Miss Pinkerton's school for young ladies before he died. He was a clever man, very friendly – usually with other drinkers – and he was often in debt. Rebecca's mother was French, a dancer in the theatre. So Rebecca spoke perfect French as it is spoken in Paris.

Her mother, and then her father, died when Rebecca Sharp was seventeen. Miss Pinkerton employed her at the school to speak French. For this she was given a few pounds a year, her bed and meals, and she could listen to the girls' lessons in her free time.

Next to most of the older girls in Miss Pinkerton's school, Rebecca Sharp looked like a child. But already she was a pupil in the school of debt and need. She had to learn to turn many debt collectors away from her father's door.

At Miss Pinkerton's school, kind Amelia Sedley was the only

person that Rebecca really liked. Then Amelia left school at the age of seventeen, and at the same time Rebecca was given the job of governess in Sir Pitt Crawley's family. So the two girls left together in the Sedleys' carriage. Rebecca was invited to stay with Amelia's family for a week before she had to leave for the Crawleys'.

The carriage begins to move. Kind Miss Jemima (the sister of Miss Pinkerton) runs after it and gives a copy of Johnson's Dictionary to Rebecca Sharp. She hopes that her sister will never know. But Miss Sharp throws her gift to the ground.

At last, Amelia and Becky arrived at the Sedleys' house in Russell Square. Amelia stopped crying and looked happy and excited. You can be sure that she showed Rebecca every room in the house, and everything in all her cupboards, and her books, and her dresses, and her piano, and two shawls. 'My brother Joseph brought them from India for me,' she told her friend.

'I would like to have a brother,' said Rebecca a little sadly. 'You must love him very much! Isn't he very rich? They say that all the men from India are rich.'

'He has plenty of money, I believe,' Amelia answered.

Chapter 2   Joseph Sedley

When it was time for dinner, the two young ladies went downstairs. A very fat man was reading the newspaper by the sitting-room fire. He stood up quickly when the young ladies went in. His face became very red.

'It's only your sister, Joseph,' said Amelia. 'I've finished school, you know. And this is my friend, Miss Sharp. You've heard me talking about her.'

'No, never, really,' said the fat man, shaking. 'Well, yes – isn't the weather cold, miss?' He attacked the fire until it burned more brightly. And this was the middle of June.

Amelia stopped crying and looked happy and excited.

'He is very good-looking,' Rebecca said quietly to Amelia.

'Do you think so?' said Amelia. 'I shall tell him.'

'No! Please don't do that!' said Miss Sharp, stepping back like a frightened woodland animal.

Joseph Sedley was twenty-nine, twelve years older than his sister Amelia, and he worked with the East India Company. He was Collector of Boggley Wollah, an important position in Bengal. But after twelve years in Boggley Wollah, he became ill and had to return to Europe.

Before his stay in India, Joseph was too young to enjoy the good life of a rich young man in London. Now he decided to enjoy it fully. He took rooms in a fashionable part of the town. He drove his horses in the park, he ate at fashionable restaurants and he went to the theatres in the tightest evening clothes. When he returned to India later, he talked all the time about his life as a fashionable young man in London. But it is true that he was as alone in London as in Boggley Wollah. He knew few people well, except his doctor. Ladies frightened him, so he almost never went to his family home in Russell Square.

At dinner, Amelia said to her brother, 'Joseph, you haven't forgotten that you promised to take me to the Royal Gardens in Vauxhall?'

'Good idea,' said old Mr Sedley, 'but each girl must have a gentleman. Why don't you send a note to number ninety-six and ask George Osborne to join you?'

Mrs Sedley looked at her husband and laughed. I don't know why she did that. Amelia looked down at the table. Her face was as red as only the face of a young lady of seventeen can be.

After dinner, to his surprise, Joseph talked easily to a young woman. Miss Rebecca asked him a great number of questions about India. He was able to tell her interesting stories about that country and his life there. His story about killing wild animals frightened her.

'Oh, Mr Sedley,' she said, 'you must never do anything so dangerous again.'

'You mustn't worry, Miss Sharp,' he said, looking quite fearless. 'The danger only makes the sport more exciting.' But all the time he thought: 'I shall not tell her that I only tried this sport once. Or that I nearly died of fear.'

Chapter 3   George Osborne and Dobbin

When Lieutenant Osborne came from 96 Russell Square to the Sedleys' house on the day of the Vauxhall party, he said to Mrs Sedley, 'I hope that you have room for Captain Dobbin of our regiment. I've asked him to come to dinner here. Then he will go with us to Vauxhall. He knows that Miss Amelia is now at home.'

'Of course,' said Mrs Sedley. 'But he is not an easy man!'

'Captain Dobbin's shyness does not matter to me,' said Amelia with a smile. 'I shall always like him, I know.' She did not give her reason for this. It was because Dobbin was a friend of George Osborne. And *he* was the most beautiful man in the British army, and the most wonderful hero.

'There isn't a finer man in the army than Dobbin,' Osborne said, 'or a better officer. But he isn't exactly good-looking.' And he looked towards the mirror at himself, at his fine moustache. He saw that Miss Sharp's green eyes were watching him. And Rebecca thought in her heart, 'Ah! I think that I understand *you*!'

That evening, Amelia came into the sitting room singing like a bird. She did not know that there was somebody already there. It was Captain William Dobbin of the Fortieth Regiment of Foot, a very tall, shy-looking gentleman. Her sweet, fresh little voice went right into the captain's heart. And that is a part of our story.

The group arrived at the Vauxhall Royal Gardens after dinner.

'Look after the shawls and things, Dobbin,' said George.

Of course our young people promised to stay together during the evening. And of course they did not. That always happens in Vauxhall. But they will meet again at supper-time and discuss their adventures.

We won't follow any of them closely on those adventures. Mr Osborne and Miss Amelia were perfectly happy, seeing everything on the main walks in the gardens. Of course Miss Rebecca Sharp and her fat friend walked along one of the side paths. The path was not well lit, and a careless visitor pushed Miss Sharp. She fell back, with a little cry of fear, into the arms of Mr Sedley. He suddenly became brave and told her some of his India stories for the sixth time.

The Vauxhall Gardens did not interest Captain Dobbin very much. He thought about joining the rest of his group at supper, but he walked past them more than once. They were sitting at a table, already talking happily. Dobbin knew that he was completely forgotten. He walked away, still carrying the young ladies' shawls.

Joseph was enjoying himself. He ordered the food and drink in a loud voice, and ate and drank most of it. At the end of the meal, he ordered a special wine. This wine was the cause, I think, of later problems. The young ladies did not drink it. Osborne did not like it. And as a result, Joseph drank nearly all of it. And as a result of that, he talked and laughed loudly. The ladies were very frightened and Mr Osborne was very angry. 'Joseph,' cried the lieutenant. 'Stop this, and let's go.' The young ladies stood up.

'Stop, my dearest, dear-dear-dear!' shouted Joseph. He was now as brave as a wild animal and took Miss Rebecca's hand. By good luck, Captain Dobbin arrived and pushed his way through the crowd. 'Where *have* you been, Dobbin?' said Osborne. He took Amelia's shawl from his friend's arm and put it round that young lady's shoulders. 'You look after Joseph, and I will take the ladies to the carriage.'

Mr Osborne and Miss Amelia were perfectly happy . . .

Chapter 4   Becky Goes to Queen's Crawley

Joseph Sedley did not come to Russell Square the next day. But on the following day he sent a note to his sister:

> Dear Amelia,
>   I was too ill to come yesterday. I am leaving London today to drink the healthy waters of Cheltenham. Please ask Miss Sharp to forgive me for last night in Vauxhall. Ask her to forgive every word. When I am better, I shall go to Scotland for some months.
>   Yours,
>   Joseph Sedley

Rebecca's hopes were at an end. Amelia did not look at her friend's pale face. She ran upstairs to cry, of course.

Soon Rebecca had to meet Sir Pitt Crawley at his town house in Great Gaunt Street and go with him to his country place, Queen's Crawley. The note from Sir Pitt was written on an old envelope:

> Great Gaunt Street
> Sir Pitt Crawley rekwests Miss Sharp and bags to be here on Tuesday. I leaf for Queens Crawley tomoro morning erly.

Rebecca said a very warm goodbye to Amelia. She took with her little presents from her friend and her friend's parents, saying, 'Oh no, Amelia, I really cannot take them!' She promised to love her friend for ever and ever and ever before she counted the money from kind Mr Sedley. Then, crying, she left. As the carriage turned the corner, Rebecca immediately dried her eyes and began to think about Sir Pitt. 'Will he wear fine clothes?' she asked herself. 'Will he be very proud? I do not think that I have ever met a baronet!'

Mr Sedley's driver stopped outside the door of Sir Pitt's tall, dark house in Great Gaunt Street. It was opened by a man in dirty old clothes, with a red face and smiling grey eyes.

'Is this the home of Sir Pitt Crawley?' the driver asked.

'It is,' said the man at the door.

'Take these bags in, then,' said the driver.

'*You* take them in.'

'I can't leave my horses! Do your job and miss will give you some beer,' said the driver, laughing. 'Miss Sharp gave nothing when she left the Sedleys' house,' he thought, laughing again.

The red-faced man took his hands out of his pockets, threw Miss Sharp's bags on his shoulder and carried them into the house. Rebecca followed him in. When he put the bags down in the dining room, she asked him, 'Where is Sir Pitt Crawley?'

'Ha, ha! *I* am Sir Pitt Crawley. And don't forget to give me some beer.'

Rebecca wrote to Amelia from Queen's Crawley. She described Sir Pitt as 'an old, short, very dirty man in old clothes and farmer's boots. He smokes a very unpleasant pipe and cooks for himself. He speaks like a farm worker, and he uses some very bad language.'

Sir Pitt *did* enjoy low life, but he was an important man at home and in all Hampshire. When he travelled, four horses always pulled his carriage. In his dining room, the food was very simple but three persons always helped at the table.

Miss Sharp was the governess to the two daughters of Sir Pitt by his second wife. By his first wife, he had two sons. One of them, Mr Pitt Crawley, was in the house. Rebecca described him to Amelia as 'pale, thin, ugly, silent; he has thin legs, no chest, pale yellow hair and a moustache'. His younger brother, Rawdon Crawley, was not at home. He was never in the house when his brother was there. They were not good friends.

Sir Pitt had an unmarried sister, Miss Crawley. She was rich –

she had seventy thousand pounds a year. So she was always very welcome at Queen's Crawley.

Miss Crawley disliked Sir Pitt's first son, but liked Rawdon. She often paid Rawdon's debts when he was at Cambridge. Now he was in the army, and she still paid them. She told everybody: 'Rawdon will get a lot of my money when I die.'

We have now met the more important persons in the family, so we must think about Rebecca. What will she do in her new life? 'I am alone in the world,' she thought. 'I must look after myself as well as I can.' So she decided to make friends with all those people who could help her.

Nobody in the house listened to Sir Pitt's wife, Lady Crawley. 'I do not need to make a friend of her,' thought Rebecca. And her daughters? Rebecca did not give them much to learn. As a result, they liked her very much.

With Mr Crawley, Miss Sharp was quiet and serious. She asked him to explain the difficult parts of French books. (But she understood them because her mother was a Frenchwoman.) And she also asked him to choose some serious books for her to read.

Mr Crawley was very pleased to help her. 'Miss Sharp is naturally good,' he thought. 'Her mother was a Montmorency, of course, one of the best families of France before the Revolution of 1789.'

After a few months at Queen's Crawley, Miss Sharp had many stories about her fine family – before the Revolution destroyed all the best families in France. Mr Crawley found some of those stories in a book on the Queen's Crawley shelves. This showed that they were true.

Rebecca read all the law papers that came to her employer at Queen's Crawley. She copied many of his letters and changed the spelling. She became interested in everything in and around Queen's Crawley – its park, its gardens, its animals. Soon Rebecca looked after the house when Mr Crawley was away.

Chapter 5   Miss Crawley

It is time now to meet Miss Crawley. She is coming to Queen's Crawley to visit her brother, Sir Pitt. We already know the most important fact about this lady: she has seventy thousand pounds a year.

You will remember that Miss Crawley disliked her brother's elder son. When she came to Queen's Crawley, he soon went away on business.

'You will understand, Miss Sharp, that my sister is not a good woman,' said Sir Pitt. 'She has an expensive house in the most fashionable part of London, and she eats and drinks too much.'

Later Miss Crawley told Rebecca, 'I enjoyed myself so much when I was young! I was very beautiful then.' (All old women were beautiful in their younger days, we know.)

This fine old lady liked Rawdon Crawley very much. She paid for him to go to Cambridge. Then when he was asked to leave the university after two years, she helped him to join the army as an officer.

Rawdon lived the life of a fashionable young man. He rode and drove a four-horse carriage in races on the roads, fought in the boxing ring and played card games. As a result of these he often had to fight other men. It was clear that he was not afraid of death.

'And he is not afraid of what follows death,' said Mr Crawley.

Miss Crawley liked Rawdon because he was brave. She always paid his debts after his fights. 'A young man who *is* a man will often be in trouble,' she said. 'He is twice as important to me as his soft too-good brother.'

Rebecca wrote to Amelia:

> Queen's Crawley has woken up. Miss Crawley has
> arrived with her fat little dog – the great and rich Miss

Crawley, with her seventy thousand pounds. She hates Mr Pitt, and so he has escaped to London.

That fashionable young man, Captain Crawley, has come. You will want to know what he is like. He is a very large young soldier – two metres tall. He speaks with a loud voice, and uses some very bad words. He shouts at everyone, but they all love him. When he has any money, he happily gives it away.

Rebecca soon won the heart of that bad old woman, Miss Crawley. One day, Sir Pitt had a big dinner party and invited all the important neighbours ...

'Is Miss Sharp not having dinner with us?' cried Miss Crawley. 'Do you think that I can talk about children with Lady Fuddleston, or law-court business with that silly old Sir Giles Wapshot? No! I want Miss Sharp to be there. She is the only person that I can enjoy talking to!'

So Miss Sharp, the governess, was ordered to have dinner with the important people in the dining room. A very serious Sir Giles walked into dinner with Miss Crawley and sat down next to her. The old lady called out loudly, 'Becky! Come and sit next to me and amuse me. Sir Giles can go and sit next to Lady Fuddleston.'

After the party, Miss Crawley said, 'Come to my room, Becky. We will talk about all the people who were at the party.' And the two new friends did this perfectly.

'You bad little thing!' Miss Crawley said. 'You must sit next to me every day at dinner. And Rawdon will sit at my other side. I like him. I want him to run away with someone, you know.'

'A rich someone, or a poor someone?'

'A rich girl, of course,' said the old lady. 'He has only the money that I give him. He has debts. He must get money and be a success in the world.'

'Is he very clever?' Rebecca asked.

Miss Crawley has arrived . . .

'Clever, my dear? He hasn't got an idea in his head except about his horses, his regiment, his riding, and his card-playing. But he will be a success because he is so beautifully bad. Everybody in his regiment loves him.'

Captain Crawley enjoyed the company of Rebecca Sharp and spoke to her like an army officer. Let's listen to them outside the house in the moonlight.

'Oh, what beautiful stars!' Miss Rebecca's eyes are looking up towards the sky and the captain's eyes are looking down towards her face. 'I feel almost unreal when I see them.'

'Oh ... ah ... yes. Exactly, Miss Sharp ... Er ... Miss Sharp, with your permission I will smoke.'

Miss Sharp loves this smell out in the garden more than anything. She smokes a little, too, in the prettiest way. She takes a little smoke into her mouth, gives a little cry – and a little laugh – and passes the dear little thing back to the captain. He pulls at his moustache. 'Ah ... yes ... aw ... a fine smoke ... aw.' He thinks and talks just like an officer.

Chapter 6   Amelia

We must now leave the countryside and travel back to Miss Amelia in London.

Captain Dobbin went to the Sedleys' house in Russell Square. He wanted to see George Osborne, of course. But he found only Amelia, sitting near the window. Her face was a little sad.

They talked about nothing at first. Then Amelia asked, 'Is it true that the Fortieth Regiment is leaving England?'

'No. Not yet.'

'Have you seen Lieutenant Osborne today?'

'He is probably with his sisters,' the captain said. 'Shall I go and get him?'

14

So she gave him her hand gratefully and he crossed the square to the Osborne house. Amelia waited and waited, but George never came.

Poor kind little heart! And so it continues to hope. Not much is happening in her life, is it? All day she thinks, 'When will he come?' I believe that George was playing cards at the time. George was a good-hearted man who loved his friends. He was very good at games.

Amelia knew nothing about what was happening in Europe. Nothing, until the war against Napoleon ended. Then her heart was happy because Lieutenant Osborne's regiment did not have to fight. Her hero was safe. Amelia believed that he was the bravest and most beautiful man in the British army, in Europe, in the world. And it is possible that Lieutenant Osborne thought so too.

'What is happening, George,' old Mr Osborne said that evening, 'between you and that little Amelia Sedley?'

'Well, I . . . ah . . . she *does* like me. You can see that.'

'And you?'

'Well, sir, didn't you order me to marry her? Don't I always do what you ask?'

The father did not look pleased. 'Yes, Sedley and I agreed the marriage. But things change. It is true that Sedley helped me in my early days in business. But I've already thanked him for that. I think Sedley's business has problems now. He lost a ship and everything in it when an American warship attacked. And the end of the war in Europe hasn't been good for his business. You can do better than marry his daughter. I must see the ten thousand pounds marriage price on the table in front of me, or you won't marry her. That's all.'

When his father said 'That's all', it was the end of the conversation. George knew that. He left the room with a cheque that old Mr Osborne wrote for him.

George Osborne changed the cheque into bank notes the next day and paid Dobbin fifty pounds. Then he went out with some other officers. That same evening, Amelia wrote a long letter to him, full of love and fears, and hopes and worries.

'Poor little Amelia,' George thought when he read it. 'Dear little Amelia. She likes me so much! And I have a terrible headache. It was the wine last night!'

Chapter 7 Becky is Married

Miss Crawley was ill. Captain Crawley rode to her London house on a fine black horse. He gave his name, and Becky came down from the sick room. She was in London to look after Miss Crawley. She put a little hand in his and took him to the dining room. And there, I am sure, they discussed the old lady's illness.

After that, the tall officer came to the house every day to talk about his aunt's health. He hoped for four thousand pounds or more.

Miss Crawley was soon feeling better and she sat up and laughed. Becky was very amusing. 'I love Miss Sharp like a daughter,' she told Rawdon.

Then, when Miss Crawley was completely better, Sir Pitt's wife died at Queen's Crawley. 'What a pity! I shall have to tell my friends not to come to my party on Friday,' said Miss Crawley. 'I hope that my brother doesn't marry again too quickly.'

'Pitt will be very angry if he does,' Rawdon laughed. He was showing his usual love for his brother.

Rebecca said nothing. She left the room before Rawdon went away. But they met near the front door and had a little talk.

The next day, Rebecca was looking out of Miss Crawley's bedroom window. She suddenly cried out, 'Here is Sir Pitt!'

'My dear,' said the old lady, 'I can't see him. I don't want to see him. Tell him that I am too ill to see anyone.'

Rebecca ran lightly down the stairs and stopped Sir Pitt from coming up. 'She is too ill to see you, sir,' she said.

'Oh, good!' Sir Pitt said. 'It is you that I want to see, Miss Becky. Come into the small sitting room.' There he looked hard at her. 'I want you back at Queen's Crawley,' he said.

'I hope to return soon,' Becky said in a low voice, 'when Miss Crawley is better. I must . . . return to . . . to the dear children.'

'You've said that for three months now, Becky. And still you stay with my sister here. She will throw you off like an old shoe when she has had enough of you. Will you come back? Yes or no?'

'I cannot. I don't think it is right . . . to be alone with you, sir,' Becky said.

'I say again, I want you.' Sir Pitt hit the table with his hand. 'I can't continue without you. The house isn't the same place. You must come back. Do come back! Dear Becky, do come.'

'Come as what, sir?' said Becky in a very soft voice.

'Come as Lady Crawley,' the baronet said. 'Will that be all right? Come back and be my wife. You're fit for it. You're more sensible than every baronet's wife in Hampshire. Will you come? Yes or no?'

'Oh, Sir Pitt!' Rebecca was nearly in tears.

'Say yes, Becky. I am an old man but a good one. I will live for twenty more years. I will make you happy – I will!' And the old man went down on his knees.

Rebecca was almost unable to think. We have never seen her lose her calm yet, but she did now. She cried some of the truest tears that ever fell from her eyes.

'Oh, Sir Pitt!' she said. 'Oh, sir . . . I . . . I am married already.'

Miss Crawley heard about this conversation and arrived in a great hurry. 'What is this?' she said to Sir Pitt. 'You have offered to marry my little friend? It isn't true, is it?'

'Yes,' said Sir Pitt.

'I have thanked Sir Pitt Crawley,' Rebecca said, 'but I can never become Lady Crawley.'

'You refused him!'

'Yes, refused,' said Rebecca sadly.

The old lady turned to Sir Pitt. 'And did you really offer to marry her?'

'Yes.'

'And she refused you?'

'Yes.' There was a bright smile on Sir Pitt's face.

Miss Crawley didn't understand. A rich old gentleman offers marriage to a governess without a penny. Then he laughs when she refuses! A governess without a penny refuses an offer of marriage from a man with four thousand pounds a year! It was a complete mystery.

There was a bright smile on Sir Pitt's face.

'You will still be my friend,' Sir Pitt told Becky as he left. 'You're a good little girl.'

Some time later, Miss Crawley learned that Miss Sharp was married to Rawdon. She cried: 'Rawdon, married? Rawdon – Rebecca – governess – nobody!' and they had to send for the doctor.

When Sir Pitt Crawley heard this news, he shouted out terrible things. It was not the kind of language that we can have on these pages. And so we will shut the door on the angry, unhappy old man.

'What will we do if the old lady doesn't forgive us?' Rawdon said to his little wife as they sat in their nice little army rooms. The new rings looked lovely on her little hands. The new shawl was beautiful. 'What will we do if she doesn't forgive us, eh, Becky?'

'Then *I* will make us rich,' she said.

'Of course,' he said, kissing her little hand. 'You can do anything.'

Chapter 8   Amelia is Married

The Sedleys' house in Russell Square is very different today. Everything inside is for sale.

You know one of the many people in the house: Captain Dobbin. He was interested in one thing only: a small square piano. Nobody wanted it, and he got it for twenty-five pounds.

John Sedley's business was not a success, so he had to sell his house and everything in it. Napoleon was now back in France. This news destroyed the business and the family.

The piano belonged to Amelia, and perhaps she will need one now. It arrived that evening at a pretty little house in Chelsea, to the west of London.

Joseph Sedley did the right thing. He wrote to his mother and told her to take money from his bankers. But he stayed in Cheltenham. There he drove his carriage, and ate and drank. And, of course, he told his stories about India.

Most people in the business houses of London soon forgot John Sedley. A few wanted him to pay his debts immediately. The most unkind of these people seemed to be John Osborne, his old friend and neighbour – the same John Osborne who was a success because of Sedley.

He wrote a short note to Amelia. The marriage plans between her and his son, Lieutenant George Osborne, were at an end. A few days later, Dobbin found Osborne in his rooms.

'Look, Dobbin. She has . . . she has sent back everything that I ever gave her.' He showed his friend a ring, a silver knife and other inexpensive things. And there was a letter:

> My father has ordered me to return these presents to you. And I must not write to you again after this. Goodbye. I only want you to be safe.
>
> I shall often play on the piano – your piano. Thank you for sending it. You are very kind.

'Where is she?' asked Osborne. 'There is no address on her letter.'

Dobbin knew. 'I saw her yesterday,' he told his friend.

'What did she say? How did she look? How was she?'

'George, she is dying,' said Dobbin.

The marriage happened because Dobbin wanted to keep Amelia alive. When he brought George to her, she changed. She grew young again and laughed and sang.

'It is almost the most painful thing that I have ever done,' he thought. But when he had to do something, Captain Dobbin always did it.

Amelia's unselfish love could soften a much harder heart than George Osborne's. 'It is so easy to make her happy,' he thought. 'But I must not see her again. No! Dobbin is right. My father will forgive me when the regiment goes to war.'

At the end of April, George and Amelia were married. When they made their marriage promises, Osborne's 'I will' came in a strong, deep, manly voice. Amelia's 'I will' came from her heart. Few people heard it except Captain Dobbin.

For the first few days after their marriage, George and Amelia chose Brighton, the fashionable seaside town on the south coast. They had rooms at the Ship Hotel, and they enjoyed themselves there quietly.

After a time, Joseph joined them. And other friends went there too. As George and Amelia came back to the hotel from a seaside walk one afternoon, they met Rebecca and her husband. Rebecca ran into the arms of her dearest friend. Crawley and Osborne shook hands.

They had a lot to talk about. Dobbin was telling George's father about the marriage, but young Osborne was a little worried about the possible result. Miss Crawley was in Brighton, resting after her illness. She refused to see Rawdon and Becky in London, so they tried to see her in Brighton.

Rawdon and Becky were also in Brighton because they had no money. Of course, nobody needs real money in Vanity Fair. But after so many meetings with debt collectors, Becky wanted a rest too.

The four friends often spent the evening together. After two or three nights, the gentlemen played a few games of cards while their wives talked. Then Joseph arrived in his fine open carriage, and he played a few games of cards with Captain Crawley. They put a little money into Rawdon's pocket.

One evening, the three gentlemen watched the London carriage come in.

'There is old Dobbin!' George cried. 'He promised to visit us in Brighton. How are you? Good to see you.'

George spoke to him alone. 'What is the news?' he asked. 'Have you seen my father? What does he say?'

Captain Dobbin looked very pale and serious. 'I've seen your father,' he said. 'How is Amelia – Mrs George? I will tell you all the news in a minute. But I've brought the greatest news of all! We're going with the army to Belgium!'

The three men were very serious at this news of war. Later that evening, Captain and Mrs Crawley discussed it.

'So, Becky, what will Mrs O do when O goes out with the regiment?'

Becky answered, 'She will cry and cry.'

'*You* won't cry, will you?'

'You bad man! Don't you know that I am coming with you? *You're* different. You're going to be one of General Tufto's officers.' This pleased her husband and he kissed the proud little head.

'Rawdon, dear,' she said. 'It is ... er ... wise to get your money from George, before he goes. Don't you agree?'

Chapter 9   Brussels

Amelia did not cry and cry. The army was going to Belgium, it is true. But nobody thought about battles. All sorts of people were following the army to Brussels and Ghent. It was like going to a great party, to another Vanity Fair. Amelia decided to go too, and Joseph. He agreed to look after her when George was away with his regiment.

The weeks in Brussels were very exciting for Joseph and he talked about them for years after that. He stopped telling his stories about India. He now had more exciting stories about adventures before, during and after the great battle of Waterloo.

For a few weeks, Amelia was really happy. George took her somewhere new every evening. He was quite pleased to do this. Then they were riding in the park one day when George said, 'That is General Tufto! So the Crawleys are here now.'

Amelia didn't understand why this news made her unhappy. The sun didn't seem to shine so brightly.

George Osborne was right. The next day, they saw a small group of the greatest men in Brussels. In the middle of the group was Rebecca. She was wearing the prettiest riding clothes and was riding a beautiful little horse.

They talked, and then went to the theatre. Rebecca Crawley sat between General Tufto and Rawdon. George had to go and speak to her there.

And so it continued, day after day, until the evening of the great dance. George got tickets for the dance from Rebecca. And so, of course, he had to leave Amelia while he went to thank Mrs Crawley. Rebecca found Amelia alone and unhappy in a corner of the room.

'Listen, Amelia,' Rebecca said, 'you must stop George playing for money. He and Rawdon play cards every night. You know that Rawdon will win every penny from him. Why don't you stop him?'

Rebecca couldn't say any more to her dear friend because George soon found her.

'Have you come to dance with me?' she said. And she left her shawl and her flowers with Amelia and went away with George. Amelia sat there, alone, and waited for the end of the evening.

At last George came back for Rebecca's shawl and flowers. He gave the flowers to her, and her eyes immediately saw the note in them. She received notes all the time now. She gave George a quick smile which said: 'I know what you have done.' Then she walked away.

George was very excited and he forgot Amelia – Dobbin found her and took her to her hotel. George went to a card table

Amelia sat there, alone, and waited for the end of the evening.

and – it seemed to be his lucky night – won quite a lot of money. Dobbin found him and took him away.

'The enemy has crossed the Sambre River,' said Dobbin, 'and our army is already fighting. We must leave in three hours.'

George went quietly to his hotel bedroom. A small light showed him Amelia's sweet, pale face. She seemed to be sleeping.

'She is so good!' he thought. 'So kind! And without friends! I have been a bad husband! I would like to change. But I know that I cannot change the past.'

He moved silently towards the sweet, pale face. Two soft, white arms closed round his neck. 'I am awake, George,' the poor child said. As she spoke, the noise of the army sounded outside. The city woke.

◆

Our fat friend, the Collector of Boggley Wollah will, of course, also stay in Brussels. Joseph was asleep when Dobbin found time for a quick visit.

'You must look after your sister,' the captain said. 'If anything happens to George, you must remember one thing. She has nobody except you to take her safely back to England. And if we do not win . . .'

'Not win?' said Joseph (but at the same time he thought, 'Perhaps the captain is not so brave after all.'). 'Not win! That is not possible, sir! But of course I will look after her.'

◆

'Becky,' Rawdon said, 'let's talk about what there is for you. Then, if I am hit . . . I've had some luck here. There is two hundred and thirty pounds. I won't take my horses: they will bring you money. And you have your little horse from the general. You can sell that.'

He put on his oldest army clothes. Then he lifted his little wife up in his arms and held her against his heart for a minute. When he put her down, there were tears in his eyes. He left.

Becky took off her pink dancing dress and a piece of paper fell out of it. She picked it up with a smile, and locked it in her box. Then she had some coffee. She looked at all the things that belonged to her, from Rawdon and from other men. There were two little gold watches – one from General Tufto and the other from George Osborne. If the worst happens, Mrs Rawdon Crawley will not do badly.

◆

When Joseph heard guns from Quatre Bras, he was wild with fear. 'We will all die!' he cried. 'I must leave Brussels. I must find horses.' But everyone was trying to leave and there were no horses. Joseph met Rebecca in the street. When she looked at his frightened face, she thought, '*He* will buy my horses.'

'Do you know where I can get horses?' Joseph asked her.

'You're not going? Who is going to look after Amelia, your poor little sister? You're not leaving her?'

'I won't leave her,' cried the frightened Collector of Boggley Wollah. 'There is a seat for her in my carriage, and one for you, dear Mrs Crawley, if you will come. And if we can get horses!'

'I will stay,' the lady said. 'But I have two horses to sell.'

Joseph nearly kissed her. They started to talk about the price. It was the most expensive half-hour of Joseph's life, but at last the business was finished.

After only six hours of the sound of guns from Quatre Bras, Joseph was glad to have the horses. 'They say that the French army is running away,' he told himself. 'But there is still the main French army under Napoleon!' And he began to shake with fear.

The guns of Waterloo began their terrible noise, much louder than the guns of Quatre Bras. It was too much for Joseph. 'I must go, Amelia,' he said. 'And you must come with me.'

'Without my husband?' Amelia said with a look of surprise. Joseph really could not listen to her. 'Goodbye, then!' he said angrily, and he ran out to his carriage.

All that day, from morning until evening, the guns sounded. It was dark when they suddenly stopped. Everybody knows the history of that day. All day the English regiments of foot soldiers stood and received the attacks of the French soldiers on horseback. Men fell, but towards evening, the attack of the French slowed down. At last, their finest regiments walked up the hill into the mouths of the English guns. On and up they came. They were near the top of the hill when the guns became too much for them. The attacking lines stopped in front of those terrible guns. Then at last the English soldiers left the hilltop. Still in their lines, they came towards the French. The French turned and ran back.

No more guns were heard in Brussels as the fighting moved far away. Darkness came down on the field and the city. And Amelia thought only of George. He was lying on his face, shot through the heart.

Chapter 10   Paris and London

A few weeks after the battle of Waterloo, a box arrived in Brighton for Miss Crawley. She already knew from the newspapers that Rawdon was brave at Waterloo, and was now a colonel. Inside the box were presents and a letter from Rawdon. The letter told Miss Crawley, in an amusing way, how Rawdon got the presents from French soldiers on the field of battle.

'Of course, I know that Rawdon can't write a letter like this,' the old lady thought. 'It is that clever little wife of his. She tells him what to say.'

She was right, of course. Becky *did* write the letter. But did

Then at last the English soldiers left the hilltop.

Miss Crawley also know that Becky bought the presents from one of the market people in Brussels?

◆

After Waterloo, Becky and Rawdon spent the winter of 1815 in Paris. They were able to do this with the money that poor Joseph Sedley paid for his two horses.

Becky's success in Paris was surprising. All the French ladies liked her. She spoke their language very well. Her husband was stupid, of course, but a stupid husband in Paris is a good thing for a wife. The gentlemen were also pleased to see her on her horse in the Bois de Boulogne. At her parties, the most famous people from Prussia, Russia, Spain and England tried to get near the amusing little lady. Paris was full of great men and women, and most of them knew Mrs Rawdon Crawley. She spent her time with the most fashionable people.

General Tufto was not very happy. Mrs Tufto was in Paris. And there were a lot of other generals round Mrs Crawley's chair or carriage. But Rawdon was enjoying himself. There were no debt collectors in Paris yet. There was plenty of card-playing, and Rawdon's luck was good.

On 26th March 1816, Rebecca had a son, little Rawdon. Miss Crawley was angrier at this news than we have ever seen her.

The old lady ordered Mr Pitt to come immediately to Brighton. There she told him, 'You *must* marry Lady Jane, the daughter of Lady Southdown, immediately.' Both Pitt and Lady Jane were good people. They always did what their parents and Miss Crawley told them. Miss Crawley also promised them money. They could have one thousand pounds a year while she was alive. Most of her money and other things were theirs when she died.

So Lady Jane became Lady Jane Crawley.

Old Miss Crawley wanted to punish Rawdon Crawley, but she made a mistake. She ordered Pitt and Lady Jane to come and live with her. But Lady Jane's mother, Lady Southdown, continued to look after her daughter in her new home, and Lady Southdown was a strong woman. She told everyone in the house to take *her* medicines and to read *her* books. Miss Crawley was now not important in her own home.

But let's hope that Lady Jane helped the frightened old lady. We can hope that she was kind to Miss Crawley in the busy battles of Vanity Fair.

We shall not see Miss Crawley again.

◆

Rawdon Crawley and his wife lived very happily and comfortably in Paris for two or three years. Rawdon left the army, but he still kept the title 'Colonel' before his name. He and Becky had no money.

Their friends enjoyed very good dinners at Mrs Crawley's table. 'How can they live so well on nothing a year?' they sometimes asked themselves. We, of course, know that this is perfectly possible in Vanity Fair.

Colonel Crawley played many games of cards and became very skilled. Like a great general, his skill became greatest when he was in most danger. Sometimes he had no luck during a game and nearly lost all his money. Then the other man, and his friends, offered to increase the amount of money that they were playing for. And then Colonel Crawley showed what a great player he was. He won, to the surprise (and cost) of the losers.

This money helped, of course. But to live so well, the Crawleys had to have debts. A few people began to worry about their money. But some good news came from England, and Mrs Crawley told everyone the news.

Colonel Crawley had a very rich aunt, Miss Crawley. He hoped for a great sum of money when she died. The news was that Miss Crawley was dying. The great colonel had to hurry away to her bedside. Mrs Crawley planned to stay in Paris until he came back.

The colonel went to Calais, for the ship to England, everybody thought. But no – he went to Brussels. Why? Because he had greater debts in London than in Paris.

The aunt, Miss Crawley, was dead, Paris learned. Mrs Crawley dressed herself and little Rawdon in black clothes. The colonel – now rich – was discussing the business of his new money. This is what Paris thought. So the Crawleys could now move to the first floor of the hotel, to more expensive rooms. Mrs Crawley and the hotel owner discussed the furniture, and soon agreed everything except the bill.

'Look after my bags and boxes very carefully,' Mrs Crawley said to the hotel owner one day. He locked the things safely away. (When he opened them, months later, there was not much in them.) And she went away in one of his carriages, with her child by her side. It was some weeks before the hotel owner discovered his mistake. From that time, he hated the English nation.

◆

Rebecca went to London to pay a small part of their many debts. In this way, she helped her husband to return home.

'He has no more money. My husband really prefers to stay in Europe. He does not want to live in England before his debts are paid . . . No, no money is coming to him . . . No, you will never get a larger amount than this.'

And so Colonel and Mrs Crawley came to London. And at their house in Curzon Street, Mayfair, they really showed their greatest skill: how to live on nothing a year.

Chapter 11 Amelia is a Mother

When the news of George's death came to the Osborne family, his sisters cried loudly. But it was worse for George's old father. You remember that Dobbin went to see old Osborne after the marriage of George and Amelia. George's father nearly lost his mind. From that time, he decided that George was not his son. George did receive two thousand pounds from his mother, but the letter added:

> Mr Osborne orders me to say that he will not receive any messages, letters or visits from you. You are not, now, his son.

'George died in battle because he refused to listen to me,' Old Osborne tried to tell himself. 'It is all because of Amelia. Why isn't *she* dead, not my son? I want to meet George again. I want to forgive him.'

Three weeks after Waterloo, Mr Osborne received a letter that was written by George before the battle.

> We are leaving in an hour for a great battle. So I want to say goodbye to you. And I am asking you to be good to my wife, and perhaps to my unborn child. I am afraid that I have already spent a large part of my mother's money. Thank you for all your kindness to me in the past. I promise you this, father. If I fall on the battlefield, I shall do it bravely. You will be proud of me.
> George.

That was all. Was George too proud or too shy? The sad old gentleman read the letter twice, then dropped it. He felt love and hate at the same time. His son was still loved but not forgiven.

Towards the end of October, Osborne said to his daughters, 'I am going abroad.' He did not tell them where he was going. But they knew. He was going to the place where George fell in battle. They also knew that Amelia was still in Brussels.

Osborne went to see the battlefield, then drove towards Brussels. Another carriage came towards him with a lady inside. An officer was riding with it. It was Major Dobbin.

The lady in the carriage was Amelia. But she was very different from the fresh young girl that Osborne remembered. Her face was white and thin. Her eyes seemed to look nowhere. As the carriages passed, her eyes looked straight at Osborne. But she did not see him. He knew her only because Dobbin was riding with the carriage. The old man hated her.

'Mr Osborne!' cried Dobbin. He rode to the carriage and held out his hand.

Osborne did not shake the hand. He shouted to the driver to hurry on. Dobbin put his hand on the side of the carriage. 'I will see you, sir,' he said. 'I have a message for you.'

'From that woman?' asked Osborne, angrily.

'No. From your son.'

'What do you want to say to me, Captain Dobbin? Or I should say *Major* Dobbin. Better men than you are dead. And you think that you can take their place!'

'Better men *are* dead,' Dobbin replied. 'I want to speak to you about one.'

'Be quick, then,' said Osborne, looking angry.

Dobbin stayed calm. 'I was his closest friend,' he said, 'and he spoke to me before the battle. Do you know how little money Amelia has?'

'I don't know her. She must go back to her father.'

Again, Dobbin stayed calm as he said: 'Mrs Osborne is ill, sir. This terrible thing has shaken her life and her mind. The doctors are very worried about her. But one thing will help her, they

33

hope. I have come to speak to you about it. She will be a mother soon. Are you going to punish the child because of the father? Or will you forgive your son's child?'

'No father in England was ever kinder to his son,' Osborne said wildly. 'And what does he do? He does not follow my clear order. He did not even say that he was wrong before his death. I promise you that I will never speak to that woman. She is not my son's wife. And that is what you can tell her!'

There was no hope there, then.

◆

A day came when poor Amelia held a child in her arms – a child with the eyes of George – a most beautiful little boy. She laughed and cried over it! She was safe. The doctors saw that there was no more danger to her life or her mind.

Dobbin brought the mother and child home to England, to her parents' house. And Dobbin went very often to the little house in Chelsea. There he spent hours talking to the Sedleys and to Amelia.

One day, Dobbin arrived in a carriage, bringing a wooden horse and other toys for little Georgy. The boy was not yet six months old.

'I've come to say goodbye, Amelia,' said the major, taking the little white hand.

'Goodbye? And where are you going?' she said.

'If you send letters to the London Regiment, they will send them to me. You are going to write to me, aren't you? I shall be away a long time.'

'I will write to you about Georgy,' she said. 'Dear William, you have been so kind to him and to me. Look at him. Isn't he wonderful?'

The little pink hands of the child closed round the honest soldier's fingers. Amelia looked up into Dobbin's face with the proud, happy look of a mother. That smile hurt him more than an unkind look. He could not speak. And then he had to say goodbye. Amelia held up her face and kissed him. 'Sssh! Don't wake Georgy!' she added, as William Dobbin went to the door with heavy steps. She didn't hear the noise of his carriage wheels as he drove away. She was looking at the child; he was laughing in his sleep.

Chapter 12   How to Live Well on Nothing a Year

If you are going to live on nothing a year in Vanity Fair, you have to have a house.

Colonel and Mrs Crawley could not buy a house in London. So they looked in a fashionable part of the town for a house that they could use for a year or two.

At one time, a Mr Raggles worked in Miss Crawley's house. Mrs Raggles was a cook in the same house. His pay was good, and he got, and saved, money in other ways. The cook left her job and opened a small fruit and vegetable shop not far from Miss Crawley's house. Then Mr Raggles also left his job. Then they added milk, butter, eggs and other fresh foods to the things that they sold in the little shop. They were soon selling milk, butter and eggs to more and more houses.

Year after year, Mr and Mrs Raggles saved more and more money until they were able to buy the house and furniture of 201 Curzon Street. Mr Raggles had to borrow some of the money from a friend, but most of it was his. They did not plan to live in a house which was so fine. But it was quite easy to find rich people to live there.

Mr Raggles was a good and happy man. With the money from the house, he could send his children to really good and expensive schools. He was born at Queen's Crawley, the son of a gardener there, and he loved the Crawley family. And the house in Curzon Street was empty when Rawdon and his wife returned to London. The old man was glad that one of the family wanted to live there.

Old Mr Raggles also helped when the Crawleys gave a dinner party. And Mrs Raggles came into the kitchen and sent wonderful dinners up to the dining room.

This, then, was how Crawley got his house for nothing. It is true that Raggles had to pay a lot of money. He had to pay for the money that he borrowed, the cost of food and drink for his family and – for a time – for the colonel, the cost of school for his children, and other things. It is true that the Raggles's happy life was completely destroyed by the Crawleys. In the end, Mr Raggles was sent to prison for debt. But somebody has to pay, even for gentlemen who live on nothing a year.

◆

The dinners at 201 Curzon Street were wonderful and always happy. The sitting rooms were very pretty, with a thousand little things that Rebecca brought from Paris. She sang at the piano to please her visitors. 'Perhaps the husband is a little stupid,' they thought, 'but his wife is the most pleasant little lady in London.'

Very soon, rich and important men began to enjoy visits to Curzon Street. Fashionable men came to Rebecca's carriage in Hyde Park. But notice that they were all men. The ladies did not look at her when they passed.

At first, Rawdon was very angry with these ladies and wanted to fight their husbands.

'No,' said Rebecca. 'You can't *shoot* me into the best houses, Rawdon dear. Remember that I was only a governess. And you, you poor silly old man, have a terrible name for debt, card games and fighting. We will have as many friends as we want after a time. But you will have to be a good boy. You must learn from your teacher.'

'I will be good,' Rawdon said. 'You, you dear, clever little thing, are the reason that I didn't go to prison in Paris!'

◆

Late one night, a party of gentlemen was sitting round the sitting-room fire in the Crawleys' house.

'Rawdon,' said Becky, 'I *must* have a sheepdog.'

'A what?' said Rawdon, looking up from the card table. Usually he thought only about his game of cards. He didn't listen to the talk except when it was about horses.

'Why do you want a sheepdog?' asked young Lord* Southdown. 'You haven't got any sheep.'

'I want a dog to look after me, to keep the wild animals off me,' said Becky, laughing. She looked up at Lord Steyne.

The great Lord Steyne was standing near the fire. He smiled. 'Can't the owner of the sheep protect his dear little sheep?' he asked.

'No,' answered Becky, laughing, 'he likes playing cards too much.'

Chapter 13   A Family in Need

Now we must find out what is happening to some friends in Chelsea. How is Amelia? What has happened to Major Dobbin? And is there any news of our friend, the Collector of Boggley Wollah?

Let's take the last person first. Joseph Sedley returned to India after his escape from Brussels. On the journey by sea, he

---

*Lord: very important men had the title *Lord* in front of their name.

saw Napoleon Bonaparte on the island of St Helena. People on Joseph's ship almost believed he was with Napoleon at the battle of Waterloo. He certainly knew a lot about Quatre Bras and Waterloo. He knew the position of every regiment and how many men were lost. He clearly *was* there because he knew so much. Perhaps in the end he really believed that he fought in the battles. He was called Waterloo Sedley during his stay in Bengal.

Joseph's bankers in London had orders to pay one hundred and twenty pounds a year to his father and mother in Chelsea. His parents had very little money now.

Amelia received fifty pounds a year from the army. 'And there is also an amount of five hundred pounds,' Dobbin said, 'that George left after his death.'

'Major Dobbin is not being honest about that,' thought old Sedley.' He told Dobbin to show him Osborne's papers immediately. Dobbin went red in the face and was more unsure of himself than ever. 'So it *is* true. He is not being honest about Amelia's money,' thought the old man.

At last Dobbin became angry and showed the old gentleman George's papers. 'You will see,' Dobbin added, 'that at the time of his death, George Osborne had less than a hundred pounds in the world. The other officers collected five hundred pounds for his wife.' This was not true. Dobbin gave every penny of the money. He also paid for Amelia's journey back to England.

'I am sorry,' the old man said. 'I was wrong – I did not believe you. Please forgive me.'

Amelia had no memory now of her husband's weak and careless ways. She remembered only the fine and beautiful hero who died bravely for his king and country. He was perfect, and the little boy, his son, was perfect too.

Miss Osborne (old Mr Osborne's eldest daughter) thought so too, when she saw Georgy at the Dobbins' house. That night, the boy came home in the Dobbins' carriage with a fine gold watch round his neck.

'There was an old lady. She cried and kissed me a lot. She is my aunt, but she isn't pretty. I don't like her. I like apples; I had a red one. I like you, Mother. The old lady gave me the watch.'

At dinner, Miss Osborne said to old Mr Osborne, 'Oh, sir! I've seen little Georgy. He is beautiful – so beautiful! And just like his father!'

The old man did not say a word. But he went very red, and his hands shook.

Chapter 14 Becky Goes Back to Queen's Crawley

Sir Pitt Crawley was very ill.

'We will have to go to Queen's Crawley, my dear,' said Mr Pitt in the house that was Miss Crawley's.

'Yes, dear,' said Lady Jane.

At Queen's Crawley he looked at his father's papers. 'We need to spend a lot of money on Queen's Crawley,' he told his wife. 'But I don't want to use my money. If he doesn't die, we have lost it.' Perhaps Pitt also thought about the time when *he* became a baronet. He could do a lot of things after his father's death.

Early one morning, Pitt Crawley was working on these papers when there was a quiet knock on the door. The nurse came in. Sir Pitt was dead.

The new Sir Pitt wrote to Rawdon. He asked his brother and Becky to come to Queen's Crawley. 'Why do I want to go to that stupid place?' Rawdon thought. 'I cannot be alone with Pitt after dinner. And horses there and back will cost us twenty pounds.'

But he took the letter to Becky. He took all his problems to her. She read the letter. Then she jumped up, crying, 'Good! Good!'

'Good?' said Rawdon. 'The old man hasn't left us any money, Becky. I had mine when I was twenty-one. You don't really want to go, do you?'

'Of course we must go, you silly old man. I want your brother to give you a seat in Parliament. And there you will help Lord Steyne. And he will get you a post as Governor in the West Indies or somewhere.'

So when the black clothes were ready, Colonel Crawley and his wife took their places in the carriage. ('We don't want to look rich,' said Becky. 'We will take a carriage with a driver and you can sit next to the driver and talk about horses.')

At Queen's Crawley, Pitt was polite to Rebecca, but Lady Jane took both Rebecca's hands and kissed her. This brought tears to Becky's eyes – a most unusual thing. Even I don't know how she did it.

After dinner, Lady Jane and Becky spent half an hour together. At the end of that time, they were the best of friends. Lady Jane told Sir Pitt later, 'Rebecca is a kind, open, friendly young woman. I like her.' Perhaps the reason for this opinion was Becky's interest in Lady Jane's two children. Perhaps it was her reply when Lady Jane said: 'I am so sorry about the way that Miss Crawley gave all her money to Pitt.'

'Dear Lady Jane, we don't mind that we are poor,' Becky replied. 'I am very glad that Miss Crawley's money can bring back the beauty of a fine old family. I am so proud to be part of that family. I am sure that Sir Pitt will use the money better than Rawdon.'

When they left Queen's Crawley, Colonel and Mrs Rawdon Crawley were very good friends with Sir Pitt Crawley and his wife.

Chapter 15   More Trouble for Amelia

Amelia received this letter from Mr Osborne.

> Mr Osborne is offering to take the boy, George
> Osborne. He will leave him all his money when Mr
> Osborne dies. He will pay you, Mrs George Osborne,
> two hundred pounds a year. You must understand that
> the child will live all the time with his grandfather.
> You, Mrs George Osborne, can see him sometimes
> here or at your house.

Amelia was not angry very often. But this time she stood up
and pulled the letter into a hundred pieces. Then she dropped
them on the floor and kicked them. 'So I must take money to
give away my child? This is not the kind of letter that a
gentleman writes. I will not answer it!'

Amelia did not know then how much trouble the little family
was in. Mr Sedley was getting very old, and his ideas were
becoming more and more childish. One business after another
lost all its money and more. The money from Joseph went
straight to a debt collector to pay the old man's debts.

When at last Amelia learned of this, she knew. Her child must
go from her – and forget her.

Amelia wrote to Miss Osborne. In simple words she told her
the reasons for this change of mind.

> My father has had more bad luck. I have too little
> money to give Georgy the life of a gentleman.

◆

With tears in her eyes, Miss Osborne showed the letter to her
father.

41

'Ah!' he said. 'So Mrs Proud has agreed? Ha, ha! I thought so!' He went to his desk, took a key from it and threw it down in front of his daughter. 'Get my son's room ready,' he said. He was laughing and crying. 'And you can send that woman some money. Send her a hundred pounds.'

'And I shall go and see her tomorrow?' Miss Osborne asked.

'Do what you like. But she isn't going to come here, you understand. I will not allow it. No, no, no! Not for all the money in London.'

'Here is some money, Father,' Amelia said, when it arrived. She kissed the old man and put a note for a hundred pounds in his hand.

Georgy wasn't too unhappy at the news. The next day at school, he told the other boys proudly: 'I am going to be rich, and have a carriage and a horse. I shall go to a finer school and I shall buy Marker's pencil case and pay the cake woman.'

Chapter 16   Becky in Trouble

At last the day came when the debt collectors caught Colonel Rawdon Crawley. They took him to prison, and from there he wrote to Rebecca:

Dear Becky,

They have got me in prison. It is the debt to Nathan – a hundred and fifty pounds. Please get the seventy pounds in my desk and offer it to Nathan. The rest must stay a debt. If you must, you can sell my watch.

Love, R.

The answer came a long time later:

Poor dear,

I am so sorry that I could not come immediately. I have a terrible headache. The doctors say that I must not leave my bed. When I am better, or before, I will get you free.

Love, Becky.

Rawdon was worried. He remembered that Sir Pitt and Lady Jane were in London. He sent a message to them. In it, he asked them to help him.

Lady Jane came. 'Pitt is at the Houses of Parliament,' she said.

The debt was quickly paid and Rawdon thanked Lady Jane a hundred times. Then he hurried home to look after Becky.

The windows of the sitting room showed that the room was full of light. 'Becky is ill,' thought Rawdon. 'I cannot understand it. Why is she not in bed?' He took out his door key and opened the front door. Someone was laughing in the sitting room. He went upstairs and listened outside the door. Then he went in.

A little table was ready with food and wine. Becky was sitting down in her evening dress. Lord Steyne had her hand in his.

Becky jumped up with a cry when she saw Rawdon's white face at the door. There was a terrible look in his eyes, and she threw herself down in front of him.

'It is not what you think, Rawdon!' she cried. 'It is not what you think!' And to Lord Steyne she said, 'Tell him that I have done nothing wrong!'

Lord Steyne thought, 'The colonel and his wife are trying to catch me!'

'Nothing wrong?' he cried. 'You, nothing wrong? I have paid for everything that you are wearing. I have given you thousands of pounds and your husband has spent it all. You are just like your mother, the dancing girl, and your husband, the card-player.'

Rawdon Crawley hit Lord Steyne twice on the face. 'You are lying, you dog!' he shouted. 'You can send your friends tomorrow. We will discuss how we will fight. Take these!' And he pulled the rings from Becky's hands and threw them at Lord Steyne.

'Come upstairs,' Rawdon said to his wife.

'Don't kill me, Rawdon,' she said.

He laughed unkindly. 'I want to see if that man is lying about the money. Has he given you any?'

'No,' said Rebecca. 'Or . . .'

'Give me your keys,' Rawdon said.

Rebecca gave him all her keys except one. It was the key of a little desk which she kept in a secret place. But Rawdon found the desk, and Rebecca had to open it. Inside were papers, old love letters – and a small case full of banknotes. Some of them were dated ten years before. One was quite new, a note for a thousand pounds from Lord Steyne.

'Did he give you this?' said Rawdon.

'Yes.'

'I shall send it to him today,' Rawdon said. 'Why didn't you give me a hundred pounds out of all this, Becky? Why didn't you?'

'I have done nothing wrong,' Becky said again. And he left her without another word.

Rebecca sat alone for hours. 'I must speak to Sir Pitt,' she thought. 'He will understand.' She walked to Great Gaunt Street – she had no money for a carriage – and she found Sir Pitt at home.

It was clear that he knew about the trouble in Curzon Street. He looked at Becky with surprise and fear.

'Oh, don't look at me like that!' cried Becky. 'I have done nothing wrong, Pitt. I promise. It is terrible. And just when . . . just when happiness was coming to us.'

'So the story in this newspaper is true?'

'Yes,' Becky said. 'Lord Steyne told me on Friday. The order has just come from the government. I asked Lord Steyne to agree to it. I know that I kept the money a secret from Rawdon. But you know that he is careless with money. You can understand why I didn't tell him about it.'

Sir Pitt was looking less worried.

Becky continued: 'I knew that Lord Steyne liked me too much. And I did try to please him in every way that an honest woman can. I wanted you, Pitt, to become a lord. Lord Steyne and I talked about it. But first, I wanted the position of Governor for Rawdon, as a surprise for him. And now it has all gone wrong! Can you help me, Pitt, dear Pitt? Please!'

◆

'I am going to kill the man,' Colonel Crawley told his friend Captain Macmurdo.

'Have you seen this in the newspaper?' Macmurdo asked. And he showed Rawdon a report:

GOVERNOR OF COVENTRY ISLAND. A warship has just arrived from Coventry Island. The Governor, Sir Thomas Liverseege, has died after an illness. Everybody on the island will miss him. The position of Governor will probably go to Colonel Rawdon Crawley, a well-known Waterloo officer.

'I haven't heard anything about that,' Rawdon said.

'It is a good job, Crawley. Three thousand a year, lovely island, excellent Government House. You can do what you like on the island. And a better job will follow it.'

Sir Pitt Crawley met them. 'You have seen the newspaper, then?' he said to Rawdon. 'Can't you try to forgive Becky?'

'She hid money from me for ten years,' Rawdon replied.

'When I found it in that desk, our marriage ended. She knew that. I will never see her again, Pitt. Never!'

There was no fight. Lord Steyne left England and did not return. The trouble was a secret that was talked about everywhere in London, and then everywhere in England, and then everywhere in the world, for a few weeks.

◆

And so the debt collectors came for poor Raggles, and he spent years in prison.

And the pretty little lady who lived in his house in Curzon Street? Where was she? Who asked after a day or two? Was she right or wrong? When we cannot decide between good or bad, Vanity Fair decides for us. We all know what that means!

Rawdon sent his wife some money. And she is, of course, a woman who needs only a little money. Young Rawdon lived happily at Queen's Crawley, and she never tried to see him.

And the new Governor of Coventry Island? *He* died of illness, but only after four years on the island.

Chapter 17   Comings and Goings

Old Sedley was sitting on a seat in the park, telling Amelia one of his old stories. He did this often now. He was getting old and his wife was dead. The little girl from the house next door came running towards them. Amelia jumped up. 'Has something happened to Georgy?' she thought.

'He has come!' called the little girl. 'Look!'

Amelia looked and saw Dobbin coming across the grass. And of course she began to cry. She ran towards him and gave him both her hands. She wasn't very different. She was a little pale, but her eyes were the same. She smiled through the tears at his honest face. Why didn't he take her in his arms and promise to stay with her for ever?

'Somebody has come with me,' he said.

'Mrs Dobbin?'

'Oh, no,' he said. 'There isn't a Mrs Dobbin. I mean your brother, Joseph. He came from India on the same ship with me. He has come home to make you all happy.'

'Father!' Amelia cried. 'Here is news! Joseph is in England. He has come to look after you.'

I am afraid that this was not completely true. But it made everybody happy.

Later, while the old man was half-asleep, Amelia had a long talk with Dobbin about her son. 'Georgy is clever. He is doing well in his new school and at his new home in Russell Square. He is so beautiful, William, so ... so like his father.' The major held her hand. 'Why can't she forget her dead husband?' he thought.

One day, Joseph's carriage came and carried old Sedley and his daughter away from Chelsea. Amelia gave nearly all her furniture to her good friends there. They took only a few dear things to their new home near Regent's Park. Dobbin was glad to see a piano – the piano.

'I am glad that you have kept it,' he said shyly to Amelia.

'Of course I have kept it. It is more important to me than anything in the world.'

'Is that true, Amelia?'

'Yes. He gave it to me.'

'I didn't know,' said poor Dobbin.

She thought about that later, when she was alone. And then at last she knew. 'It was William who gave me the piano, not George!' she cried. The pain was terrible.

Old Mr Sedley's last illness continued for many months, but Old Mr Osborne's was short. Before his death he changed his mind about Amelia.

Young George Osborne liked Major Dobbin. And because of that, his grandfather, old Mr Osborne, saw Dobbin quite often. Mr Osborne's opinion of the soldier was completely different since their meeting in Brussels. More than once, he asked the major about Mrs George Osborne. The major could talk easily about that subject. 'You don't know what she suffered, sir,' said honest Dobbin. 'I hope that you will be kind to her. She took your son away from you – that is true. But she gave hers to you. I know how much you loved your George. You can be sure that she loves her little Georgy ten times more.'

'You are a good man,' Old Osborne said. Four days later he was dead, two days after Old Sedley. Mr Osborne left most of his money to Georgy. He asked Major Dobbin to look after it while Georgy was a boy. But five hundred pounds a year went to Georgy's mother, 'the wife of my dear son, George Osborne'.

Chapter 18   In Europe

Joseph Sedley became worried again about his health. He decided to visit towns in Europe where the healthy waters were famous. Many British people were visiting these towns at the time. Joseph took with him his sister Amelia and her son. Georgy's 'uncle' Dobbin could not go, but he often visited them.

In the town of Pumpernickel, there was a great dance, with a room at one side for card games. One evening, when nobody was looking, Georgy Osborne went into this room. It was very exciting. He was watching one game when a pretty lady lost all her money. Part of her face was covered. She saw the boy looking at her, and she said, 'Will you do something for me?' She took some money out of a little bag. 'Please play this for me. Put it on any number. You will have beginner's luck.'

Georgy laughed and put the money on number fifteen. Number fifteen won. 'Thank you,' said the pretty lady. Then Dobbin and Joseph came looking for George. Dobbin took the boy away, but Joseph stayed. He sat down next to the lady and started to play.

'Are you playing to win?' the lady asked.

'No.'

'I play to forget ... But I can't. I can't forget old times. Your sister's child is just like his father. But you haven't changed.'

'What? Who are you?' cried Joseph, very worried.

'Have you forgotten me, Joseph Sedley?' She uncovered her face.

Joseph said very softly, 'Mrs Crawley!'

'Rebecca,' she said, putting her hand on his. 'I am staying at the Elephant Hotel. Ask for Madame de Raudon.'

What was Becky's life until then? She moved from one place to another in Europe. She had only Colonel Rawdon's three hundred pounds a year. So she had to go to the places where English people go. And after a time, somebody always arrived who knew her. Then people started talking about her and she had to leave. It was not a good life.

The day after the meeting at the play table, Joseph dressed even more finely than usual and went to the Elephant Hotel. It was not one of the best hotels. He and Becky had a long and very friendly talk. At the end of it, Joseph thought: 'It is clear that she liked me all those years ago! And she has never stopped thinking about me!'

'She hasn't a friend in the world,' Joseph told Amelia after that meeting. That was too much for the soft-hearted Amelia. She wanted to help. 'Oh, the poor thing, she has really suffered!' she said. 'Becky must come here.'

She uncovered her face.

'Don't have her in the house!' said Dobbin, when Amelia told him.

'I am surprised at you, Major William!' cried Amelia. 'We must help her now, when she is so unhappy.'

'She was not always your friend,' said Dobbin. 'Not in Brussels.'

Amelia was angry – in a way that we have only seen once before. 'I shall never forgive you, never,' she said. 'You have hurt my memories of George.' Then she walked out of the room.

It was the end of everything for Dobbin. He did not come to dinner with Amelia, Joseph, George and Rebecca. After dinner, Georgy was at the window. 'Look!' he said. 'There is Dob's little carriage, and they are carrying his bags out to it. Is he going anywhere?'

'Yes,' said Amelia, 'he is going on a journey.'

'And when is he coming back?' Georgy wanted to know.

'He is . . . is not coming back,' answered Amelia.

◆

The rich people were leaving Pumpernickel. It was time to move to a place by the sea. Joseph's doctor, too, was going to Ostend for the sea air. He wanted Joseph to go there – the doctor was making a lot of money out of Joseph's illnesses. Joseph couldn't decide what to do. But then Rebecca offered to go to Ostend with him. And, of course, Joseph paid for her move.

At Ostend, Amelia was very kind to Becky. Becky's heart seemed to become kinder too. 'Listen to me, Amelia,' said Becky. 'I want to talk to you. You are like a baby in arms. You cannot live in this world alone. You must have a husband, you silly girl. And you turned away one of the best men in the world, you silly, heartless, thankless little thing!'

'I tried . . . I tried to love him, Rebecca,' said Amelia, 'but I couldn't forget . . .' She looked up at the picture of George.

'Couldn't forget *him*!' cried Becky. 'That dishonest man who thought only of himself! That stupid, heartless man! I'm telling you, he didn't want to marry you. But Dobbin told him to keep his promise. George told me that. He laughed about you to me. He even made love to me the week after he married you.'

'It isn't true! It isn't true!' cried Amelia.

'Not true?' Becky said, still kindly. 'Look at this, then, you silly girl.' She took a piece of paper from her dress, opened it, and put it in Amelia's hands. 'You know his writing. He wrote that to me. He wanted me to run away with him the day before he died.'

Amelia looked at the letter. It was the one from Becky's flowers at the dance in Brussels. Amelia's head fell, and for almost the last time in this story, she began to cry. Was she crying because George was not her hero now? Or were they tears of happiness because now she could love with all her heart?

Rebecca was kind to her and kissed her – a very unusual thing for Mrs Crawley. 'And now,' Becky said, 'let's get a pen and paper. You must ask him to come immediately.'

'I ... I wrote to him this morning,' Amelia said, her face very red.

◆

Becky was not at the marriage of her dear friends, but she was kind to the lonely and ill Joseph Sedley. She travelled everywhere with him until the day he died. He left half his money to Amelia and half to his dear friend Rebecca. She now lives in England and goes to church very often, and helps at many church fairs.

And the family never speaks of her.

ACTIVITIES

Chapters 1–5

Before you read

1 Read the Introduction to the book. Then discuss what you have learnt about *Vanity Fair*. Where did the title of the book come from? What kind of place is Vanity Fair? How do people act there?

2 The story starts at the beginning of the 1800s. Becky Sharp is seventeen years old. Her parents are dead and she has no money or relatives. What problems will she have in life? What skills will she need? What do you think?

3 Look at the Word List at the back of the book.

   a Find words that are useful in a story about the army.

   b Find words that are useful in a story about rich, fashionable people.

While you read

4 What do you learn about Becky Sharp? Is this information about Becky (✓) or about a different person (✗)?

   a happy to own a copy of Johnson's Dictionary   .....
   b parents are dead; has to find a way to live   .....
   c speaks perfect French and has a job as a governess   .....
   d a shy, fat, lonely Collector   .....
   e a tall, shy, helpful captain in the army   .....
   f wears dirty old clothes and has four children   .....
   g Sir Pitt Crawley's oldest child   .....
   h lives very well in London on seventy thousand pounds .....
   i well-liked by people   .....
   j Miss Crawley's favourite relative   .....
   k helps Sir Pitt with his letters and business   .....

After you read

5 Look at the information in Question 4 that is *not* about Becky Sharp. Who is each piece of information about?

6 a How does Becky Sharp meet each of these people?

Amelia Sedley   Joseph Sedley   George Osborne
Sir Pitt Crawley   Sir Pitt's daughters   Miss Crawley
Rawdon Crawley

b What does Becky think of these people? What is their opinion of her?

7 Work with another student. Have one of these conversations. Use your imagination.

a *Student A*:   You are Becky Sharp on your first evening at the Sedleys' house on Russell Square. Ask Joseph Sedley about his time in India.

Student B: You are Joseph Sedley. Tell Becky some interesting stories about India and your life there.

b *Student A*:   You are Miss Crawley. You are visiting Queen's Crawley, and Captain Rawdon Crawley returns home. Ask him questions about his latest adventures.

Student B: Answer your aunt's questions.

Chapters 6–9

Before you read

8 How do people find a husband or wife in your country? How do you think they find one in the world of *Vanity Fair*?

9 Rawdon Crawley, George Osborne and William Dobbin are young officers in the army. Do young men and women in your country often choose a life in the army? Is it a good life, do you think? Why (not)?

10 Who says these words? Who are they talking to? Complete the table.

		Speaker	Listener
a	'Have you seen Lieutenant Osborne today?'		
b	'You can do better than marry his daughter.'		
c	'I love Miss Sharp like a daughter.'		
d	'Oh, sir . . . I . . . I am married already.'		
e	'Of course. You can do anything.'		
f	'George, she is dying.'		
g	'*You* won't cry, will you?'		
h	'Have you come to dance with me?'		
i	'You must look after your sister.'		
j	'But I have two horses to sell.'		

After you read

11 Discuss what is happening during the conversations in Question 10.

12 Amelia goes to all of these places. Why? What happens there?

    a the Sedleys' house on Russell Square

    b the Sedleys' new house in Chelsea

    c Brighton

    d Belgium

13 Work with another student. What does the storyteller really want to tell the reader with these sentences?

    a 'And it is possible that Lieutenant Osborne thought so too.' (Chapter 6)

    b 'And there, I am sure, they discussed the old lady's illness.' (Chapter 7)

    c 'He was showing his usual love for his brother.' (Chapter 7)

    d 'Of course, nobody needs real money in Vanity Fair.' (Chapter 8)

    e 'Amelia didn't understand why this news made her unhappy.' (Chapter 9)

Chapters 10–13

Before you read

14 Use books or the Internet to find some facts about Napoleon Bonaparte. What were his great successes? What happened to him after the Battle of Waterloo?

15 Which people from the story are alive and still in Belgium at the end of Chapter 9? How will these people's lives be different after the Battle of Waterloo?

While you read

16 Are these sentences right (✓) or wrong (✗)?

    a Rawdon Crawley buys some gifts for his aunt and writes an amusing letter to her. .....

    b Becky Sharp is more intelligent than her husband. .....

    c Miss Crawley orders Mr Pitt Crawley to marry Lady Jane. .....

    d Becky and Rawdon are very sad when they hear the news about Miss Crawley's serious illness. .....

    e Becky leaves many unpaid debts behind when she leaves Paris. .....

    f Old Mr Osborne cannot forgive George for his marriage to Amelia Sedley. .....

    g Captain William Dobbin dies at the Battle of Waterloo. .....

h Becky and Rawdon Crawley are good, kind
friends to Mr and Mrs Raggles. .....

i The ladies from the best London families accept
Becky as their close friend. .....

j Joseph Sedley is able to help his parents. .....

k George Osborne's sister has a beautiful son too. .....

After you read

17 Explain why:

   a Becky is a success in Paris for two or three years.

   b Mr Pitt Crawley marries Lady Jane.

   c Rawdon Crawley goes to Brussels and not to London.

   d the hotel owner in Paris hates the English nation.

   e old Mr Osborne hates Amelia.

   f William Dobbin tries to help Amelia before Georgy's birth.

   g the Crawleys are able to live in Raggles's house.

   h Joseph Sedley is called 'Waterloo Sedley' in Bengal.

   i Old Mr Osborne doesn't want to hear from his daughter about
young Georgy, his grandson.

18 Work with another student. Have one of these conversations.

   a *Student A*: You are Mr Raggles, in prison. Answer the other
prisoner's questions.

      Student B: You are in prison too, because you robbed a bank.
Ask Mr Raggles about his life. Why is he in prison?
You want to know everything about his story.

   b *Student A*: You are a fashionable lady in London. You live near
Colonel and Mrs Rawdon Crawley, but you do not
visit Mrs Crawley. Talk to a friend in a different city
about Becky.

      Student B: You want to know about Mrs Rawdon Crawley.
Ask your friend questions about her.

Chapters 14–18

Before you read

19 Who is your favourite person in the story? Why do you like him or her?

20 Choose two people from the story. How do you think the story will end for them? Will they be happy or not?

While you read

21 Circle the correct words.

    a Pitt Crawley has *very little / a lot of* money after his father dies.

    b Becky is *happy / unhappy* about going to Queen's Crawley after the old man's death.

    c Becky and Rawdon don't want their carriage to look too *expensive / inexpensive* on their visit to Queen's Crawley.

    d Lady Jane and Becky have *an unfriendly / a very friendly* talk together.

    e Amelia is *very angry / very happy* when she receives a letter from Mr Osborne.

    f Amelia has to give Georgy to Mr Osborne because the Sedleys have problems with *their neighbours / money.*

    g Georgy is *excited / sad* about living with his grandfather.

22 Complete these sentences.

    a Rawdon Crawley is taken to _____ because he can't pay his debts.

    b _____ pays Rawdon's debt to Nathan.

    c Lord Steyne has given Becky a lot of _____.

    d Rawdon becomes _____ of Coventry Island.

    e Rawdon never sees his wife and _____ again.

    f Dobbin returns to Amelia's house with _____.

    g Amelia has always believed that _____ gave her the piano.

    h Mr Osborne dies and leaves most of his money to _____.

    i The night before the battle near Brussels, George wanted to run away with _____.

    j At last, _____ marries Amelia, the woman he has always loved.

23 What happens next?

    a Becky and Rawdon learn that Sir Pitt is dead.

    b The new Sir Pitt and his wife have dinner with Rawdon and Becky at Queen's Crawley.

    c Amelia's father has more business problems and loses more money.

    d Lady Jane pays Rawdon's debt, and he leaves prison.

    e Old Mr Osborne dies.

    f Joseph Sedley goes to Ostend for the sea air.

    g Becky tells Amelia some surprising things about her husband, George.

    h Joseph Sedley dies.

24 Work with another student. People can be described in different ways. Discuss these questions about the people in this story:

    a How is Becky Sharp a good friend and a bad friend to Amelia Sedley and to Joseph Sedley?

    b How is Becky a good wife and a bad wife to Rawdon Crawley?

    c How is Rawdon Crawley a good husband and a bad husband?

    d How is George Osborne a good husband and a bad husband?

    e How is William Dobbin a good friend and a bad friend to George Osborne?

    f How is old Mr Osborne a good father and a bad father to his son, George? How is he a good grandfather and a bad grandfather to Georgy?

Writing

25 Imagine that you are Miss Pinkerton. Becky Sharp helps students at your school with their French. She is now looking for a job. Write a letter for her to show to possible employers. In what ways is Becky a good worker?

26 Compare Becky Sharp and Amelia Sedley. Think about their families, their lives at school, their husbands, their actions towards other people in the story and their futures.

27 Imagine that you are Amelia Sedley, the new Mrs George Osborne. Write two postcards to your mother: one on your second day in Brighton, and one at the end of your second week in Brighton.

28 Write two short newspaper reports from the battlefield at Waterloo – one for a British newspaper and one for an English-language French newspaper.

29 Young Georgy Osborne, the son of George and Amelia Osborne, is now fifteen years old and he wants to know more about his father. Write a conversation between him and Major William Dobbin, his father's old friend.

30 Write Mrs Amelia Osborne's letter to George Osborne at the end of Chapter 6, or her letter to William Dobbin at the end of Chapter 18.

31 Imagine that Rawdon Crawley dies in battle and George Osborne does not. Write a different ending to *Vanity Fair*.

32 Imagine that you are William Dobbin. You are now happily married to Amelia. Write a page in your private notebook about your new life.

33 Thackeray called *Vanity Fair* a story without a hero. Write about two important people in the story. Why can we *not* call them heroes or heroines?

34 Explain Thackeray's use of a storyteller to attack rich and important people in his book.

Answers for the Activities in this book are available from the Penguin Readers website. A free Activity Worksheet is also available from the website. Activity Worksheets are part of the Penguin Teacher Support Programme, which also includes Progress Tests and Graded Reader Guidelines. For more information, please visit: www.penguinreaders.com.

WORD LIST

army (n) the group of all the soldiers in a country

baronet (n) a title given by the king or queen. After a man's death, the title passes to his son.

battle (n) a fight between soldiers in war

captain (n) an army officer who gives orders to a group of soldiers

carriage (n) a passenger vehicle pulled by one or more horses

collect (v) to bring things together from different places

colonel (n) a very important army officer

debt (n) money that you have to pay to a person or business

fair (n) something like a market in a field or a park. People buy things, win things and have fun.

fashionable (adj) popular for a short time

general (n) one of the highest and most important officers in the army

gentleman (n) a polite man who acts well towards other people

hero/heroine (n) the most important man/woman in a story. A hero or heroine is a good or brave person.

governess (n) a female teacher who lives at a family home and teaches the children there

lieutenant (n) an army officer with a position lower than a captain

major (n) an army officer with a position higher than a captain but lower than a colonel

regiment (n) a large group of soldiers, made from a number of smaller groups

revolution (n) a fight for a completely different kind of government

shawl (n) a piece of clothing that women wear round their shoulders

vanity (n) the state of being too proud of yourself

Silas Marner
George Eliot

Silas Marner loves only one thing – his money. Each night he takes it out from his hiding place and counts it. Then two things happen to change his life – his gold coins are stolen and a little girl comes to live with him. Slowly, Silas Marner starts to change.

David Copperfield
Charles Dickens

David Copperfield's happy life suddenly changes when his mother marries again. Her new husband sends him away to school. When his mother dies, David is sent to work in London, but he runs away. His life of adventure, love and friendship has begun.

Billy Elliot
Melvin Burgess

Eleven-year-old Billy Elliot is different from other boys. He is not very clever or good at sport. Then, one day, he discovers ballet dancing. Finally he has found something that he can do well. But everybody knows that ballet is for girls, not boys! Will Billy continue to dance? Or have his father and brother got other plans for him?